*

*I will praise and give Thanks to the LORD
with all my Heart
and speak of all thy marvelous Miracles.*

(Psalm 9, 2)

*Translation
by Martin Luther*

*

Signs, Wonders and Miracles
in the Bible

Testimonies from the Old and New Testament

Bibliografische Information der Deutschen Nationalbibliothek:
Die Deutsche Nationalbibliothek verzeichnet diese Publikation in der Deutschen Nationalbibliografie: detaillierte bibliografische Daten sind im Internet über http://dnb.dnb.de abrufbar.

TWENTYSIX – Der Self-Publishing-Verlag
Eine Kooperation zwischen der Verlagsgruppe Random House und BoD – Books on Demand

Herstellung und Verlag:
BoD – Books on Demand, Norderstedt

ISBN: 978-3-740-78232-0

Translation: **Douay-Rheims 1899**

Layout, Schriftsatz, Formatierung:
Antonia Katharina Tessnow
www.antonia-katharina.de

Content

Before the Exodus from Egypt	*8*
The ten Plagues over Egypt	*12*
Signs and Wonders during the Procession through the Desert	*32*
During the Time of the Landgrap	*60*
During the Time of Samuel	*64*
During the Time of the Kings	*66*
Under Eliah	*80*
Under Eliseus	*94*
During the Time of the Babylonian Exile	*114*
From the New Testament	*120*
Register	*146*
Thanks	*148*
About the Author	*150*
Further Publications	*151*

For with God nothing shall be impossible.

Luke 1, 37

Before the Exodus from Egypt

The burning Bush

Exodus 3, 1 - 3

Now Moses fed the sheep of Jethro his father in law, the priest of Madian: and he drove the flock to the inner parts of the desert, and came to the mountain of God, Horeb.

And the Lord appeared to him in a flame of fire out of the midst of a bush: and he saw that the bush was on fire and was not burnt.

And Moses said: 'I will go and see this great sight, why the bush is not burnt.'

Moses Rod is turned into a Serpent and back into a Rod

Exodus 4, 2 - 5

Then he said to him: 'What is that thou holdest in thy hand?'

He answered: 'A rod.'

And the Lord said: 'Cast it down upon the ground.'

He cast it down, and it was turned into a serpent: so that Moses fled from it. And the Lord said: 'Put out thy hand and take it by the tail.'

He put forth his hand, and took hold of it, and it was turned into a rod.

'That they may believe', saith he, 'that the Lord God of their fathers, the God of Abraham, the God of Isaac, and the God of Jacob, hath appeared to thee.'

Moses Hand becomes leprous and whole again

Exodus 4, 6 - 7

And the Lord said again: 'Put thy hand into thy bosom.'

And when he had put it into his bosom, he brought it forth leprous as snow.

And he said: 'Put back thy hand into thy bosom.'

He put it back, and brought it out again, and it was like the other flesh.

The ten Plagues of Egypt

Mose's Rod becomes a Serpent

Exodus 7, 8 - 12

And the Lord said to Moses and Aaron: 'When Pharao shall say to you, shew signs: thou shalt say to Aaron: Take thy rod, and cast it down before Pharao, and it shall be turned into a serpent.'

So Moses and Aaron went in unto Pharao, and did as the Lord had commanded. And Aaron took the rod before Pharao, and his servants, and it was turned into a serpent.

And Pharao called the wise men and the magicians: and they also by Egyptian enchantments and certain secrets did in like manner.

And they every one cast down their rods, and they were turned into serpents: but Aaron's rod devoured their rods.

Water turned into Blood

Exodus 7, 17 - 23

Thus therefore saith the Lord: 'In this thou shalt know that I am the Lord: behold I will strike with the rods that is in my hand, the water of the river, and it shall be turned into blood. And the fishes that are in the river shall die, and the waters shall be corrupted, and the Egyptians shall be afflicted when they drink the water of the river.'

The Lord also said to Moses: 'Say to Aaron, - Take thy rod, and stretch forth thy hand upon the waters of Egypt, and upon their rivers, and streams and pools, and all the ponds of waters, that they may be turned into blood: and let blood be in all the land of Egypt, both in vessels of wood and of stone. -'

And Moses and Aaron did as the Lord had commanded: and lifting up the rod he struck the water of the river before Pharao and his servants: and it was turned into blood.

And the fishes that were in the river died: and the river corrupted, and the Egyptians could not drink the water of the river, and there was blood in all the land of Egypt.

And the magicians of the Egyptians with their enchantments did in like manner: and Pharao's heart was hardened, neither did he hear them, as the Lord had commanded.

And he turned himself away and went into his house, neither did he set his heart to it this time also.

The Plague of the Frogs

Exodus 8, 1 - 15

And the Lord said to Moses: 'Go in to Pharao, and thou shalt say to him: Thus saith the Lord: Let my people go to sacrifice to me. But if thou wilt not let them go behold I will strike all thy coasts with frogs. And the river shall bring forth an abundance of frogs: which shall come up, and enter into thy house, and thy bedchamber, and upon thy bed, and in the houses of thy servants, and to thy people, and into thy ovens, and into the remains of thy meats; And the frogs shall come in to thee and to thy people, and to all thy servants.'

And the Lord said to Moses: 'Say to Aaron, Stretch forth thy hand upon the streams and upon the rivers and the pools, and bring forth frogs upon the land of Egypt.'

And Aaron stretched forth his hand upon the waters of Egypt, and the frogs came up, and covered the land of Egypt.

And the magicians also by their enchantments did in like manner, and they brought forth frogs upon all the land of Egypt.

But Pharao called Moses and Aaron and said to them: 'Pray ye to the Lord to take away the frogs from me and from my people; and I will let the people go to sacrifice to the Lord.'

And Moses said to Pharao: 'Set me a time when I shall pray for thee, and for thy servants, and for thy people, that the frogs may be driven away from thee and from thy house, and from thy servants, and from thy people: and may remain only in the river.'

And he answered: 'To morrow.'

But he said: 'I will do according to thy word; that thou mayst know that there is none like to the Lord our God. And the frogs shall depart from thee, and from thy house, and from thy servants, and from thy people; and shall remain only in the river.'

And Moses and Aaron went forth from Pharao: and Moses cried to the Lord for the promise, which he had made to Pharao concerning the frogs.

And the Lord did according to the word of Moses: and the frogs died out of the houses, and out of the villages, and out of the fields: And they gathered them together into immense heaps, and the land was corrupted.

And Pharao seeing that rest was given, hardened his own heart, and did not hear them, as the Lord had commanded.

The Plague of the Sciniphs

Exodus 8, 16 - 19

And the Lord said to Moses: 'Say to Aaron, Stretch forth thy rod, and strike the dust of the earth: and may there be sciniphs in all the land of Egypt.

And they did so. And Aaron stretched forth his hand, holding the rod: and he struck the dust of the earth, and there came sciniphs on men and on beasts: all the dust of the earth was turned into sciniphs through all the land of Egypt.

And the magicians with their enchantments practiced in like manner, to bring forth sciniphs, and they could not and there were sciniphs as well on men as on beasts. And the magicians said to Pharao: 'This is the finger of God.'

And Pharao heart was hardened, and he hearkened not unto them, as the Lord had commanded.

The Plague of the Flies

Exodus 8, 20 - 32

The Lord also said to Moses: 'Arise early, and stand before Pharao: for he will go forth to the waters: and thou shalt say to him: Thus saith the Lord: Let my people go to sacrifice to me. But if thou wilt not let them go, behold I will send in upon thee, and upon thy servants, and upon thy houses all kind of flies: and the houses of the Egyptians shall be filled with flies of divers kinds, and the whole land wherein they shall be.

And I will make the land of Gessen wherein my people is, wonderful in that lay, so that flies shall not be there: and thou shalt know that I am the Lord in the midst of the earth. And I will put a division between my people and thy people: to morrow shall this sign be.'

And the Lord did so.

And there came a very grievous swarm of flies into he houses of Pharao and of his servants, and into all the land of Egypt: and the land was corrupted by this kind of flies.

And Pharao called Moses and Aaron, and said to them: 'Go, and sacrifice to your God in this land.'

And Moses said: 'It cannot be so: for we shall sacrifice the abominations of the Egyptians to the Lord our God: now if we kill those things which the Egyptians worship, in their presence, they will stone us. We will go three days' journey into the wilderness: and we will sacrifice to the Lord our God, as he hath commanded us.'

And Pharao said: 'I will let you go to sacrifice to the Lord your God in the wilderness: but go no farther: pray for me.'

And Moses said: 'I will go out from thee, and will pray to the Lord: and the flies shall depart from Pharao, and from his servants, and from his people to morrow: but do not deceive any more, in not letting the people go to sacrifice to the Lord.'

So Moses went out from Pharao, and prayed to the Lord.

And he did according to his word: and he took away the flies from Pharao, and from his servants, and from his people: there was not left so much as one.

And Pharao's heart was hardened, so that neither this time would he let the people go.

The Plague of the Beasts

Exodus 9, 1 - 7

And the Lord said to Moses: 'Go in to Pharao, and speak to him: Thus saith the Lord God of the Hebrews: Let my people go to sacrifice to me. But if thou refuse, and withhold them still: Behold my hand shall be upon thy fields: and a very grievous murrain upon thy horses, and asses, and camels, and oxen, and sheep.

And the Lord will make a wonderful difference between the possessions of Israel and the possessions of the Egyptians, that nothing at all shall die of those things that belong to the children of Israel.'

And the Lord appointed a time, saying: 'To morrow will the Lord do this thing in the land.'

The Lord therefore did this thing the next day: and all the beasts of the Egyptians died, but of the beasts of the children of Israel there died not one.

And Pharao sent to see: and there was not any thing dead of that which Israel possessed. And Pharao's heart was hardened, and he did not let the people go.

The Plague of the Blains

Exodus 9, 8 - 12

And the Lord said to Moses and Aaron: 'Take to you handfuls of ashes out of the chimney, and let Moses sprinkle it in the air in the presence of Pharao. And be there dust upon all the land of Egypt: for there shall be boils and swelling blains both in men and beasts in the whole land of Egypt.'

And they took ashes out of the chimney, and stood before Pharao, and Moses sprinkled it in the air: and there came boils with swelling blains in men and beasts.

Neither could the magicians stand before Moses for the boils that were upon them, and in all the land of Egypt.

And the Lord hardened Pharao's heart, and he hearkened not unto them, as the Lord had spoken to Moses.

The Plague of the Hail

Exodus 9, 13 - 28

And the Lord said to Moses: 'Arise in the morning, and stand before Pharao, and thou shalt say to him: Thus saith the Lord the God of the Hebrews: Let my people go to sacrifice to me. For I will at this time send all my plagues upon thy heart, and upon thy servants, and upon thy people: that thou mayst know there is none like me in all the earth. For now I will stretch out my hand to strike thee, and thy people with pestilence, and thou shalt perish from the earth.

And therefore have I raised thee, that I may shew my power in thee, and my name may be spoken of throughout all the earth. Dost thou yet hold back my people: and wilt thou not let them go?

Behold I will cause it to rain to morrow at this same hour, an exceeding great hail: such as hath not been in Egypt from the day that it was founded, until this present time. Send therefore now presently, and gather together thy cattle, and all that thou hast in the field: for men and beasts, and all things that shall be found abroad, and not gathered together out of the fields, which the hail shall fall upon, shall die.'

He that feared the word of the Lord among

Pharao's servants, made his servants and his cattle flee into houses: But he that regarded not the word of the Lord, left his servants and his cattle in the fields:

And the Lord said to Moses: 'Stretch forth thy hand towards heaven, that there may be hail in the whole land of Egypt, upon men, and upon beasts, and upon every herb of the field in the land of Egypt.'

And Moses stretched forth his rod towards heaven, and the Lord sent thunder and hail, and lightning running along the ground: and the Lord rained hail upon the land of Egypt.

And the hail and fire mixed with it drove on together: and it was of so great bigness, as never before was seen in the whole land of Egypt since that nation was founded.

And the hail destroyed through all the land of Egypt all things that were in the fields, both man and beast: and the hail smote every herb of the field, and it broke every tree of the country. Only in the land of Gessen, where the children of Israel were, the hail fell not.

And Pharao sent and called Moses and Aaron, saying to them: 'I have sinned this time also; the Lord is just: I and my people are wicked. Pray ye to the Lord, that the thunderings of God and the hail may cease: that I may let you go, and that you may stay here no longer.'

The Plague of the Locust

Exodus 10, 3 - 20

Therefore Moses and Aaron went in to Pharao, and said to him: 'Thus saith the Lord God of the Hebrews: How long refusest thou to submit to me? let my people go, to sacrifice to me. But if thou resist, and wilt not let them go, behold I will bring in to morrow the locust into thy coasts: To cover the face of the earth that nothing thereof may appear, but that which the hail hath left may be eaten: for they shall feed upon all the trees that spring in the fields.

And they shall fill thy houses, and the houses of thy servants, and of all the Egyptians: such a number as thy fathers have not seen, nor thy grandfathers, from the time they were first upon the earth, until this present day.'

And he turned himself away, and went forth from Pharao.

And Pharao's servants said to him: 'How long shall we endure this scandal? let the men go to sacrifice to the Lord their God. Dost thou not see that Egypt is undone?'

And they called back Moses and Aaron to Pharao: and he said to them: 'Go, sacrifice to the Lord your God: who are they that shall go?'

Moses said: 'We will go with our young and old, with our sons and daughters, with our sheep and herds: for it is the solemnity of the Lord our God.'

And Pharao answered: 'So be the Lord with you, as I shall let you and your children go: who can doubt but that you intend some great evil? It shall not be so: but go ye men only, and sacrifice to the Lord: for this yourselves also desired.'

And immediately they were cast out from Pharao's presence.

And the Lord said to Moses: 'Stretch forth thy hand upon the land of Egypt unto the locust, that it may come upon it, and devour every herb that is left after the hail.'

And Moses stretched forth his rod upon the land of Egypt: and the Lord brought a burning wind all that day, and night: and when it was morning, the burning wind raised the locusts: And they came up over the whole land of Egypt: and rested in all the coasts of the Egyptians innumerable, the like as had not been before that time, nor shall be hereafter. And they covered the whole face of the earth, wasting all things. And the grass of the earth was devoured, and what fruits soever were on the trees, which the hail had left: and there remained not any thing that was green on the trees, or in the herbs of the earth in all Egypt.

Wherefore Pharao in haste called Moses and Aaron, and said to them: 'I have sinned against the Lord your God, and against you. But now forgive me my sin this time also, and pray to the Lord your God, that he take away from me this death.'

And Moses going forth from the presence of Pharao, prayed to the Lord. And he made a very strong wind to blow from the west, and it took the locusts and cast them into the Red Sea: there remained not so much as one in all the coasts of Egypt.

And the Lord hardened Pharao's heart, neither did he let the children of Israel go.

Three Days of Darkness

Exodus 19, 21 - 29

And the Lord said to Moses: 'Stretch out thy hand towards heaven: and may there be darkness upon the land of Egypt, so thick that it may be felt.'

And Moses stretched forth his hand towards heaven: and there came horrible darkness in all the land of Egypt for three days. No man saw his brother, nor moved himself out of the place where he was: but wheresoever the children of Israel dwelt there was light.

And Pharao called Moses and Aaron, and said to them: 'Go sacrifice to the Lord: let your sheep only, and herds remain; let your children go with you.'

Moses said: 'Thou shalt give us also sacrifices and burnt offerings, to the Lord our God. All the flocks shall go with us: there shall not a hoof remain of them: for they are necessary for the service of the Lord our God: especially as we know not what must be offered, till we come to the very place.'

And the Lord hardened Pharao's heart, and he would not let them go.

And Pharao said to Moses: 'Get thee from me, and beware thou see not my face any more: in what day soever thou shalt come in my sight, thou shalt die.'

Moses answered: 'So shall it be as thou hast spoken, I will not see thy face any more.'

Death of the Firstborn

Exodus 12, 29 - 32

And it came to pass at midnight, the Lord slew every firstborn in the land of Egypt, from the firstborn of Pharao, who sat on his throne, unto the firstborn of the captive woman that was in the prison, and all the firstborn of cattle.

And Pharao arose in the night, and all his servants, and all Egypt: for there was not a house wherein there lay not one dead.

And Pharao calling Moses and Aaron, in the night, said: 'Arise and go forth from among my people, you and the children of Israel: go, sacrifice to the Lord as you say. Your sheep and herds take along with you, as you demanded, and departing, bless me.'

*Signs and Wonders
during the Procession
through the Desert*

A Pillar of Cloud and a Pillar of Fire

Exodus 13, 21 - 22

And the Lord went before them to shew the way by day in a pillar of a cloud, and by night in a pillar of fire: that he might be the guide of their journey at both times. There never failed the pillar of the cloud by day, nor the pillar of fire by night, before the people.

Numbers 9, 15 - 23

Now on the day that the tabernacle was reared up, a cloud covered it. But from the evening there was over the tabernacle, as it were, the appearance of fire until the morning. So it was always: by day the cloud covered it, and by night as it were the appearance of fire. And when the cloud that covered the tabernacle was taken up, then the children of Israel marched forward: and in the place where the cloud stood still, there they camped.

At the commandment of the Lord they marched, and at his commandment they pitched the tabernacle. All the days that the cloud abode over the tabernacle, they remained in the same place: And if it was so that it continued over it a long time, the children of Israel kept the watches of the Lord, and marched not, for as many days soever as the cloud stayed over the tabernacle.

At the commandment of the Lord they pitched their tents, and at his commandment they took them down. If the cloud tarried from evening until morning, and immediately at break of day left the tabernacle, they marched forward: and if it departed after a day and a night, they took down their tents.

But if it remained over the tabernacle for two days or a month or a longer time, the children of Israel remained in the same place, and marched not: but immediately as soon as it departed, they removed the camp.

By the word of the Lord they pitched their tents, and by his word they marched: and kept the watches of the Lord according to his commandment by the hand of Moses.

Division of the Sea

Exodus 14, 21 - 31

And when Moses had stretched forth his hand over the sea, the Lord took it away by a strong and burning wind blowing all the night, and turned it into dry ground: and the water was divided. And the children of Israel went in through the midst of the sea dried up: for the water was as a wall on their right hand and on their left.

And the Egyptians pursuing went in after them, and all Pharao's horses, his chariots and horsemen through the midst of the sea, and now the morning watch was come, and behold the Lord looking upon the Egyptian army through the pillar of fire and of the cloud, slew their host. And overthrew the wheels of the chariots, and they were carried into the deep. And the Egyptians said: 'Let us flee from Israel: for the Lord fighteth for them against us.'

And the Lord said to Moses: 'Stretch forth they hand over the sea, that the waters may come again upon the Egyptians, upon their chariots and horsemen.'

And when Moses had stretched forth his hand towards the sea, it returned at the first break of day to the former place: and as the Egyptians were fleeing away, the waters came upon them, and the Lord shut them up in the middle of the waves. And the waters returned, and covered the chariots and the horsemen of all the army of Pharao, who had come into the sea after them, neither did there so much as one of them remain.

But the children of Israel marched through the midst of the sea upon dry land, and the waters were to them as a wall on the right hand and on the left: And the Lord delivered Israel on that day out of the hands of the Egyptians.

And they saw the Egyptians dead upon the sea shore, and the mighty hand that the Lord had used against them: and the people feared the Lord, and they believed the Lord, and Moses his servant.

The Waters of Mara turn sweet

Exodus 15, 22 - 25

And Moses brought Israel from the Red Sea, and they went forth into the wilderness of Sur: and they marched three days through the wilderness, and found no water. And they came into Mara, and they could not drink the waters of Mara, because they were bitter: whereupon he gave a name also agreeable to the place, calling it Mara, that is, bitterness.

And the people murmured against Moses, saying: 'What shall we drink?'

But he cried to the Lord, and he shewed him a tree, which when he had cast into the waters, they were turned into sweetness.

Divine Exaltation
through the Contribution of Quails and Manna

Exodus 16, 11 - 15

And the Lord spoke to Moses, saying:

'I have heard the murmuring of the children of Israel: say to them: In the evening you shall eat flesh, and in the morning you shall have your fill of bread: and you shall know that I am the Lord your God.'

So it came to pass in the evening, that quails coming up, covered the camp: and in the morning, a dew lay round about the camp. And when it had covered the face of the earth, it appeared in the wilderness small, and as it were beaten with a pestle, like unto the hoar frost on the ground.

And when the children of Israel saw it, they said one to another: 'Manhu!' which signifieth: 'What is this!' for they knew not what it was.

And Moses said to them: 'This is the bread, which the Lord hath given you to eat.'

Feeding with Manna

Exodus 16, 16 - 36

This is the word, that the Lord hath commanded: 'Let every one gather of it as much as is enough to eat: a gomor for every man, according to the number of your souls that dwell in a tent, so shall you take of it.'

And the children of Israel did so: and they gathered, one more, another less. And they measured by the measure of a gomor: neither had he more that had gathered more: nor did he find less that had provided less: but every one had gathered, according to what they were able to eat.

And Moses said to them: 'Let no man leave thereof till the morning.'

And they hearkened not to him, but some of them left until the morning, and it began to be full of worms, and it putrified, and Moses was angry with them.

Now every one of them gathered in the morning, as much as might suffice to eat: and after the sun grew hot, it melted. But on the sixth day they gathered twice as much, that is, two gomors every man: and all the rulers of the multitude came, and told Moses. And he said to them: 'This is what the Lord hath spoken: To morrow is the rest of the sabbath sanctified to the Lord. Whatsoever work is to be done, do it: and the meats that are to be dressed, dress them: and whatsoever shall remain, lay it up until the morning.'

And they did so as Moses had commanded, and it did not putrify, neither was there worm found in it. And Moses said: 'Eat it to day, because it is the sabbath of the Lord: to day it shall not be found in the field. Gather it six days: but on the seventh day is the sabbath of the Lord, therefore it shall not be found.'

And the seventh day came: and some of the people going forth to gather, found none. And the Lord said to Moses: 'How long will you refuse to keep my commandments, and my law? See that the Lord hath given you the sabbath, and for this reason on the sixth day he giveth you a double provision: let each man stay at home, and let none go forth out of his place the seventh day.'

And the people kept the sabbath on the seventh day. And the house of Israel called the name thereof Manna: and it was like coriander seed white, and the taste thereof like to flour with honey.

And Moses said: 'This is the word, which the Lord hath commanded: Fill a gomor of it, and let it be kept unto generations to come hereafter, that they may know the bread, wherewith I fed you in the wilderness, when you were brought forth out of the land of Egypt.'

And Moses said to Aaron: 'Take a vessel, and put manna into it, as much as a gomor can hold: and lay it up before the Lord to keep unto your generations, as the Lord commanded Moses.'

And Aaron put it in the tabernacle to be kept.

And the children of Israel ate manna forty years, till they came to a habitable land: with this meat were they fed, until they reached the borders of the land of Chanaan.

Now a gomor is the tenth part of an ephi.

Water out of the Rock Horeb

Exodus 17, 1 - 7

Then all the multitude of the children of Israel setting forward from the desert of Sin, by their mansions, according to the word of the Lord, encamped in Raphidim, where there was no water for the people to drink. And they chode with Moses, and said: 'Give us water, that we may drink.'

And Moses answered them: 'Why chide you with me? Wherefore do you tempt the Lord?'

So the people were thirsty there for want of water, and murmured against Moses, saying: 'Why didst thou make us go forth out of Egypt, to kill us and our children, and our beasts with thirst?'

And Moses cried to the Lord, saying: 'What shall I do to this people? Yet a little more and they will stone me.'

And the Lord said to Moses: 'Go before the people, and take with thee of the ancients of Israel: and take in thy hand the rod wherewith thou didst strike the river, and go. Behold I will stand there before thee, upon the rock Horeb: and thou shalt strike the rock, and water shall come out of it that the people may drink.'

Moses did so before the ancients of Israel

Victory against Amalec through Moses' lifted Arms

Exodus 17, 8 - 16

And Amalec came, and fought against Israel in Raphidim. And Moses said to Josue: 'Choose out men: and go out and fight against Amalec: to morrow I will stand on the top of the hill having the rod of God in my hand.'

Josue did as Moses had spoken, and he fought against Amalec; but Moses, and Aaron, and Hur went up upon the top of the hill. And when Moses lifted up his hands, Israel overcame: but if he let them down a little, Amalec overcame.

And Moses' hands were heavy: so they took a stone, and put under him, and he sat on it: and Aaron and Hur stayed up his hands on both sides. And it came to pass that his hands were not weary until sunset. And Josue put Amalec and his people to flight, by the edge of the sword.

And the Lord said to Moses: 'Write this for a memorial in a book, and deliver it to the ears of Josue: for I will destroy the memory of Amalec from under heaven.'

And Moses built an altar: and called the name thereof, The Lord my exaltation, saying:

'Because the hand of the throne of the Lord, and the war of the Lord shall be against Amalec, from generation to generation.'

Moses Face shone

Exodus 34, 29 - 35

And it came to pass, when Moses came down from mount Sinai — and the two tables of testimony were in Moses' hand, when he came down from the mountain — that Moses knew not that the skin of his face shone through his talking with him. And Aaron and all the children of Israel saw Moses, and behold, the skin of his face shone; and they were afraid to come near him.

And Moses called to them; and they turned to him, — Aaron and all the principal men of the assembly; and Moses talked with them.

And afterwards, all the children of Israel came near; and he gave them in commandment all that Jehovah had spoken with him on mount Sinai. And Moses ended speaking with them; and he had put on his face a veil.

And when Moses went in before Jehovah to speak with him, he took the veil off, until he came out; and he came out, and spoke to the children of Israel what he was commanded.

And the children of Israel saw the face of Moses, that the skin of Moses' face shone; and Moses put the veil on his face again, until he went in to speak with him.

(Darby Translation)

Nadab and Abihu dying before the LORD

Leviticus 10, 1 - 2

And Nadab and Abiu, the sons of Aaron, taking their censers, put fire therein, and incense on it, offering before the Lord strange fire: which was not commanded them.

And fire coming out from the Lord destroyed them, and they died before the Lord.

Fire in Tabhera

Numbers 11, 1 - 2

In the mean time there arose a murmuring of the people against the Lord, as it were repining at their fatigue. And when the Lord heard it he was angry. And the fire of the Lord being kindled against them, devoured them that were at the uttermost part of the camp.

And when the people cried to Moses, Moses prayed to the Lord, and the fire was swallowed up.

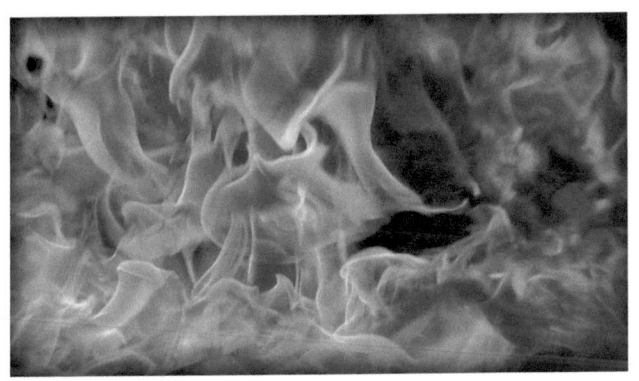

70 Man prophesiesed

Numbers 11, 25 - 29

And the Lord came down in a cloud, and spoke to him, taking away of the spirit that was in Moses, and giving to the seventy men. And when the spirit had rested on them they prophesied, nor did they cease afterwards.

Now there remained in the camp two of the men, of whom one was called Eldad, and the other Medad, upon whom the spirit rested; for they also had been enrolled, but were not gone forth to the tabernacle.

And when they prophesied in the camp, there ran a young man, and told Moses, saying: 'Eldad and Medad prophesy in the camp.'

Forthwith Josue the son of Nun, the minister of Moses, and chosen out of many, said: 'My lord Moses forbid them.'

But he said: 'Why hast thou emulation for me? O that all the people might prophesy, and that the Lord would give them his spirit!'

Quails are brought in Kibroth-Hattaawa

Numbers 11, 31 - 34

And a wind going out from the Lord, taking quails up beyond the sea brought them, and cast them into the camp for the space of one day's journey, on every side of the camp round about, and they flew in the air two cubits high above the ground.

The people therefore rising up all that day, and night, and the next day, gathered together of quails, he that did least, ten cores: and they dried them round about the camp.

As yet the flesh was between their teeth, neither had that kind of meat failed: when behold the wrath of the Lord being provoked against the people, struck them with an exceeding great plague.

And that place was called, *The graves of lust*: for there they buried the people that had lusted. And departing from the graves of lust, they came unto Haseroth, and abode there.

Core, Dathan and Abiron were swallowed by the Earth

Numbers 16, 28 - 35

And Moses said: 'By this you shall know that the Lord hath sent me to do all things that you see, and that I have not forged them of my own head: If these men die the common death of men, and if they be visited with a plague, wherewith others also are wont to be visited, the Lord did not send me.

But if the Lord do a new thing, and the earth opening her mouth swallow them down, and all things that belong to them, and they go down alive into hell, you shall know that they have blasphemed the Lord.'

And immediately as he had made an end of speaking, the earth broke asunder under their feet: And opening her mouth, devoured them with their tents and all their substance. And they went down alive into hell the ground closing upon them, and they perished from among the people.

But all Israel, that was standing round about, fled at the cry of them that were perishing: saying: 'Lest perhaps the earth swallow us up also.'

And a fire coming out from the Lord, destroyed the two hundred and fifty men that offered the incense.

Aarons Rod bloomed, blossomed and formed Almonds

Numbers 17, 1 - 8

And the Lord spoke to Moses, saying:

'Speak to the children of Israel, and take of every one of them a rod by their kindreds, of all the princes of the tribes, twelve rods, and write the name of every man upon his rod. And the name of Aaron shall be for the tribe of Levi, and one rod shall contain all their families:

And thou shalt lay them up in the tabernacle of the covenant before the testimony, where I will speak to thee. Whomsoever of these I shall choose, his rod shall blossom: and I will make to cease from me the murmurings of the children of Israel, wherewith they murmur against you.'

And Moses spoke to the children of Israel: and all the princes gave him rods one for every tribe: and there were twelve rods besides the rod of Aaron.

And when Moses had laid them up before the Lord in the tabernacle of the testimony: He returned on the following day, and found that the rod of Aaron for the house of Levi, was budded: and that the buds swelling it had bloomed blossoms, which spreading the leaves, were formed into almonds.

Water from the Rock in Meriba

Numbers 20, 6 - 11

And Moses and Aaron leaving the multitude, went into the tabernacle of the covenant, and fell flat upon the ground, and cried to the Lord, and said: 'O Lord God, hear the cry of this people, and open to them thy treasure, a fountain of living water, that being satisfied, they may cease to murmur.'

And the glory of the Lord appeared over them. And the Lord spoke to Moses, saying: 'Take the rod, and assemble the people together, thou and Aaron thy brother, and speak to the rock before them, and it shall yield waters. And when thou hast brought forth water out of the rock, all the multitude and their cattle shall drink.'

Moses therefore took the rod, which was before the Lord, as he had commanded him, And having gathered together the multitude before the rock, he said to them: 'Hear, ye rebellious and incredulous: Can we bring you forth water out of this rock?'

And when Moses had lifted up his hand, and struck the rock twice with the rod, there came forth water in great abundance, so that the people and their cattle drank.

The fiery Serpents and the brazen Serpent

Numbers 21, 4 - 9

And they marched from mount Hor, by the way that leadeth to the Red Sea, to compass the land of Edom. And the people began to be weary of their journey and labour: And speaking against God and Moses, they said: 'Why didst thou bring us out of Egypt, to die in the wilderness? There is no bread, nor have we any waters: our soul now loatheth this very light food.'

Wherefore the Lord sent among the people fiery serpents, which bit them and killed many of them. Upon which they came to Moses, and said: 'We have sinned, because we have spoken against the Lord and thee: pray that he may take away these serpents from us.'

And Moses prayed for the people.

And the Lord said to him: 'Make brazen serpent, and set it up for a sign: whosoever being struck shall look on it, shall live.'

Moses therefore made a brazen serpent, and set it up for a sign: which when they that were bitten looked upon, they were healed.

During the Time of the Landgrap

The Jordan was dipped in Part

Joshua 3, 14 - 17

So the people went out of their tents, to pass over the Jordan: and the priests that carried the ark of the covenant. went on before them. And as soon as they came into the Jordan, and their feet were dipped in part of the water, (now the Jordan, it being harvest time, had filled the banks of its channel,) The waters that came down from above stood in one place, and swelling up like a mountain, were seen afar off from the city that is called Adom, to the place of Sarthan: but those that were beneath, ran down into the sea of the wilderness (which now is called the Dead Sea) until they wholly failed.

And the people marched over against Jericho: and the priests that carried the ark of the covenant of the Lord, stood girded upon the dry ground in the midst of the Jordan, and all the people passed over through the channel that was dried up.

The Walls of Jericho fell down

Joshua 6, 20

So all the people making a shout, and the trumpets sounding, when the voice and the sound thundered in the ears of the multitude, the walls forthwith fell down: and every man went up by the place that was over against him: and they took the city.

Sun and Moon stood still in Gabaon

Joshua 10, 12 - 14

Then Josue spoke to the Lord, in the day that he delivered the Amorrhite in the sight of the children of Israel, and he said before them: 'Move not, O sun, toward Gabaon, nor thou, O moon, toward the valley of Ajalon.'

And the sun and the moon stood still, till the people revenged themselves of their enemies. Is not this written in the book of the just? So the sun stood still in the midst of heaven, and hasted not to go down the space of one day.

There was not before nor after so long a day, the Lord obeying the voice of a man, and fighting for Israel.

During the Time of Samuel

The Stump of Dagon is dis-empowered

1. Samuel 5, 1 - 5

And the Philistines took the ark of God, and carried it from the Stone of help into Azotus. And the Philistines took the ark of God, and brought it into the temple of Dagon, and set it by Dagon.

And when the Azotians arose early the next day, behold Dagon lay upon his face on the ground before the ark of the Lord: and they took Dagon, and set him again in his place.

And the next day again, when they rose in the morning, they found Dagon lying upon his face on the earth before the ark of the Lord: and the head of Dagon, and both the palms of his hands were cut off upon the threshold:

And only the stump of Dagon remained in its place. For this cause neither the priests of Dagon, nor any that go into the temple tread on the threshold of Dagon in Azotus unto this day.

During the Time of the Kings

God struck Oza

2. Samuel 6, 6 - 8

And when they came to the floor of Nachon, Oza put forth his hand to the ark of God, and took hold of it: because the oxen kicked and made it lean aside.

And the indignation of the Lord was enkindled against Oza, and he struck him for his rashness: and he died there before the ark of God.

Jeroboams Altar rips;
his Hand withered and was restored

1. Kings 13, 3 - 6

And he gave a sign the same day, saying: 'This shall be the sign, that the Lord hath spoken: Behold the altar shall be rent, and the ashes that are upon it shall be poured out.'

And when the king had heard the word of the man of God, which he had cried out against the altar in Bethel, he stretched forth his hand from the altar, saying: 'Lay hold on him.'

And his hand which he stretched forth against him withered: and he was not able to draw it back again to him.

The altar also was rent, and the ashes were poured out from the altar, according to the sign which the man of God had given before in the word of the Lord.

And the king said to the man of God: 'Entreat the face of the Lord thy God, and pray for me, that my hand may be restored to me.'

And the man of God besought the face of the Lord, and the king's hand was restored to him, and it became as it was before.

Ozia is beaten with Leprosy

2. Chronicles 26, 19

And Ozias was angry, and holding in his hand the censer to burn incense, threatened the priests. And presently there rose a leprosy in his forehead before the priests, in the house of the Lord at the altar of incense.

The Angel of the LORD beats the Assyrians

2. Kings 19, 35

And it came to pass that night, that an angel of the Lord came, and slew in the camp of the Assyrians a hundred and eighty-five thousand. And when he arose early in the morning, he saw all the bodies of the dead.

2. Chronicles 32, 20 - 21

And Ezechias the king, and Isaias the prophet the son of Amos, prayed against this blasphemy, and cried out to heaven.

And the Lord sent an angel who cut off all the stout men and the warriors, and the captains of the army of the king of the Assyrians.

The dying Ezechias was healed

2. Kings 20, 1 - 7

In those days Ezechias was sick unto death: and Isaias the son of Amos the prophet came and said to him: 'Thus saith the Lord God: Give charge concerning thy house, for thou shalt die, and not live.'

And he turned his face to the wall, and prayed to the Lord, saying: 'I beseech thee, O Lord, remember how I have walked before thee in truth, and with a perfect heart, and have done that which is pleasing before thee.'

And Ezechias wept with much weeping.

And before Isaias was gone out of the middle of the court, the word of the Lord came to him, saying: 'Go back, and tell Ezechias the captain of my people: Thus saith the Lord the God of David thy father: I have heard thy prayer, and I have seen thy tears: and behold I have healed thee; on the third day thou shalt go up to the temple of the Lord. And I will add to thy days fifteen years: and I will deliver thee and this city out of the hand of the king of the Assyrians, and I will protect this city for my own sake, and for David my servant's sake.'

And Isaias said: 'Bring me a lump of figs.'

And when they had brought it, and laid it upon his boil. he was healed.

The Miracle Sign of the Shadow

2. Kings 20, 8 - 11

And Ezechias had said to Isaias: 'What shall be the sign that the Lord will heal me, and that I shall go up to the temple of the Lord the third day?'

And Isaias said to him: 'This shall be the sign from the Lord, that the Lord will do the word which he hath spoken: Wilt thou that the shadow go forward ten lines, or that it go back so many degrees?'

And Ezechias said: 'It is an easy matter for the shadow to go forward ten lines: and I do not desire that this be done, but let it return back ten degrees.'

And Isaias the prophet called upon the Lord, and he brought the shadow ten degrees backwards by the lines, by which it had already gone down in the dial of Achaz.

Isaiah 38

In those days Ezechias was sick even to death, and Isaias the son of Amos the prophet came unto him, and said to him: 'Thus saith the Lord: Take order with thy house, for thou shalt die, and not live.'

And Ezechias turned his face toward the wall, and prayed to the Lord, And said: 'I beseech thee, O Lord, remember how I have walked before thee in truth, and with a perfect heart, and have done that which is good in thy sight.' And Ezechias wept with great weeping.

And the word of the Lord came to Isaias, saying: 'Go and say to Ezechias: Thus saith the Lord the God of David thy father: I have heard thy prayer, and I have seen thy tears: behold I will add to thy days fifteen years: And I will deliver thee and this city out of the hand of the king of the Assyrians, and I will protect it.

And this shall be a sign to thee from the Lord, that the Lord will do this word which he hath spoken: Behold I will bring again the shadow of the lines, by which it is now gone down in the sun dial of Achaz with the sun, ten lines backward. And the sun returned ten lines by the degrees by which it was gone down.'

***

The writing of Ezechias king of Juda, when he had been sick, and was recovered of his sickness. I said: 'In the midst of my days I shall go to the gates of hell: I sought for the residue of my years.'

I said: 'I shall not see the Lord God in the land of the living. I shall behold man no more, nor the inhabitant of rest.

My generation is at an end, and it is rolled away from me, as a shepherd's tent. My life is cut off, as by a weaver: whilst I was yet but beginning, he cut me off: from morning even to night thou wilt make an end of me.

I hoped till morning, as a lion so hath he broken all my bones: from morning even to night thou wilt make an end of me. I will cry like a young swallow, I will meditate like a dove: my eyes are weakened looking upward: Lord, I suffer violence, answer thou for me.

What shall I say, or what shall he answer for me, whereas he himself hath done it? I will recount to thee all my years in the bitterness of my soul.

O Lord, if man's life be such, and the life of my spirit be in such things as these, thou shalt correct me, and make me to live.

Behold in peace is my bitterness most bitter: but thou hast delivered my soul that it should not perish, thou hast cast all my sins behind thy back. For hell shall not confess to thee, neither shall death praise thee: nor shall they that go down into the pit, look for thy truth. The living, the living, he shall give praise to thee, as I do this day: the father shall make thy truth known to the children.

O Lord, save me, and we will sing our psalms all the days of our life in the house of the Lord.'

Now Isaias had ordered that they should take a lump of figs, and lay it as it plaster upon the wound, and that he should be healed.

Jonas is swallowed by a big Fish and spit him back out

Jonah 2

Now the Lord prepared a great fish to swallow up Jonas: and Jonas was in the belly of the fish three days and three nights. And Jonas prayed to the Lord his God out of the belly of the fish. And he said: 'I cried out of my affliction to the Lord, and he heard me: I cried out of the belly of hell, and thou hast heard my voice.

And thou hast cast me forth into the deep in the heart of the sea, and a flood hath compassed me: all thy billows, and thy waves have passed over me. And I said: I am cast away out of the sight of thy eyes: but yet I shall see thy holy temple again.

The waters compassed me about even to the soul: the deep hath closed me round about, the sea hath covered my head. I went down to the lowest parts of the mountains: the bars of the earth have shut me up for ever: and thou wilt bring up my life from corruption, O Lord my God.

When my soul was in distress within me, I remembered the Lord: that my prayer may come to thee, unto thy holy temple. They that are vain observe vanities, forsake their own mercy. But I with the voice of praise will sacrifice to thee: I will pay whatsoever I have vowed for my salvation to the Lord.'

And the Lord spoke to the fish: and it vomited out Jonas upon the dry land.

God lets an Ivy grow and wither

Jonah 4, 6 - 7

And the Lord God prepared an ivy, and it came up over the head of Jonas, to be a shadow over his head, and to cover him (for he was fatigued): and Jonas was exceeding glad of the ivy.

But God prepared a worm, when the morning arose on the following day: and it struck the ivy and it withered.

Under Eliah

Rain is held back

1. Kings 17, 1 - 6

And Elias the Thesbite of the inhabitants of Galaad said to Achab: 'As the Lord liveth the God of Israel, in whose sight I stand, there shall not be dew nor rain these years, but according to the words of my mouth.'

And the word of the Lord came to him, saying: 'Get thee hence, and go towards the east and hide thyself by the torrent of Carith, which is over against the Jordan, And there thou shalt drink of the torrent: and I have commanded the ravens to feed thee there.'

So he went, and did according to the word of the Lord: and going, he dwelt by the torrent Carith, which is over against the Jordan.

And the ravens brought him bread and flesh in the morning, and bread and flesh in the evening, and he drank of tile torrent.

At the Widows House of Sarephta neither Meal nor Oil was diminished

1. Kings 17, 8 - 16

Then the word of the Lord came to him, saying: 'Arise, and go to Sarephta of the Sidonians, and dwell there: for I have commanded a widow woman there to feed thee.

He arose, and went to Sarephta. And when he was come to the gate of the city, he saw the widow woman gathering sticks, and he called her, and said to her: 'Give me a little water in a vessel, that I may drink.'

And when she was going to fetch it he called after her, saying: 'Bring me also, I beseech thee, a morsel of bread in thy hand.'

And she answered: 'As the Lord thy God liveth, I have no bread, but only a handful of meal in a pot, and a little oil in a cruse: behold I am gathering two sticks that I may go in and dress it, for me and my son, that we may eat it, and die.'

And Elias said to her: 'Fear not, but go, and do as thou hast said: but first make for me of the same meal a little hearth cake, and bring it to me: and after make for thyself and thy son. For thus saith the Lord the God of Israel: The pot of meal shall not waste, nor the cruse of oil be diminished, until the day wherein the Lord will give rain upon the face of the earth.'

She went and did according to the word of Elias: and he ate, and she, and her house: and from that day the pot of meal wasted not, and the cruse of oil was not diminished, according to the word of the Lord, which he spoke in the hand of Elias.

The Son of the Widow is brought back to Life

1. Kings 17, 17 - 24

And it came to pass after this that the son of the woman, the mistress of the house, fell sick, and the sickness was very grievous, so that there was no breath left in him. And she said to Elias: 'What have I to do with thee, thou man of God? art thou come to me that my iniquities should be remembered, and that thou shouldst kill my son?'

And Elias said to her: 'Give me thy son.'

And he took him out of her bosom, and carried him into the upper chamber where he abode, and laid him upon his own bed.

And he cried to the Lord, and said: 'O Lord my God, hast thou afflicted also the widow, with whom I am after a so maintained, so as to kill her son?'

And he stretched, and measured himself upon the child three times, and cried to the Lord, and said: 'O Lord my God, let the soul of this child, I beseech thee, return into his body.'

And the Lord heard the voice of Elias: and the soul of the child returned into him, and he revived.

And Elias took the child, and brought him down from the upper chamber to the house below, and delivered him to his mother, and said to her: Behold thy son liveth. And the woman said to Elias: 'Now, by this I know that thou art a man of God, and the word of the Lord in thy mouth is true.'

God answers to Elisas Prayer with Fire

1. Kings 18, 36 - 39

And when it was now time to offer the holocaust, Elias the prophet came near and said: 'O Lord God of Abraham, and Isaac, and Israel, shew this day that thou art the God of Israel, and I thy servant, and that according to thy commandment I have done all these things.

Hear me, O Lord, hear me: that this people may learn, that thou art the Lord God, and that thou hast turned their heart again.'

Then the fire of the Lord fell, and consumed the holocaust, and the wood, and the stones, and the dust, and licked up the water that was in the trench.

And when all the people saw this, they fell on their faces, and they said: The Lord he is God, the Lord he is God.

Elias prays for Rain

1. Kings 18, 41 - 45

And Elias said to Achab: 'Go up, eat, and drink: for there is a sound of abundance of rain.'

Achab went up to eat and drink: and Elias went up to the top of Carmel, and casting himself down upon the earth put his face between his knees, And he said to his servant: 'Go up, and look toward the sea.'

And he went up, and looked, and said: 'There is nothing.'

And again he said to him: 'Return seven times.'

And at the seventh time, behold, a little cloud arose out of the sea like a man's foot. And he said: 'Go up and say to Achab: Prepare thy chariot and go down, lest the rain prevent thee.'

And while he turned himself this way and that way, behold the heavens grew dark, with clouds, and wind, and there fell a great rain.

Elias ran before Ahabs Chariot to Jezrahel

1. Kings 18, 46

And the hand of the Lord was upon Elias, and he girded up his loins and ran before Achab, till he came to Jezrahel.

Elias divides the Jordan

2. Kings 2, 8

And Elias took his mantle and folded it together, and struck the waters, and they were divided hither and thither, and they both passed over on dry ground.

Elias demands Fire from Heaven

2. Kings 1, 9 - 15

And he sent to him a captain of fifty, and the fifty men that were under him. And he went up to him, and as he was sitting on the top of a hill, said to him: 'Man of God, the king hath commanded that thou come down.'

And Elias answering, said to the captain of fifty: 'If I be a man of God, let fire come down from heaven, and consume thee, and thy fifty.'

And there came down fire from heaven, and consumed him, and the fifty that were with him.

And again he sent to him another captain of fifty men, and his fifty with him. And he said to him: 'Man of God, thus saith the king: Make haste and come down.'

Elias answering, said: 'If I be a man of God, let fire come down from heaven, and consume thee and thy fifty.'

And fire came down from heaven, and consumed him and his fifty.

Again he sent a third captain of fifty men, and the fifty that were with him. And when he was come, he fell upon his knees, before Elias, and besought him and said: 'Man of God, despise not my life, and the lives of thy servants that are with me. Behold fire came down from heaven, and consumed the two first captains of fifty men, and the fifties that were with them: but now I beseech thee to spare my life.'

And the angel of the Lord spoke to Elias, saying: 'Go down with him, fear not.'

He arose therefore, and went down with him to the king.

Elias goes up to Heaven

2. Kings 2, 11 - 12

And as they went on, walking and talking together, behold a fiery chariot, and fiery horses parted them both asunder: and Elias went up by a whirlwind into heaven.

And Eliseus saw him, and cried: 'My father, my father, the chariot of Israel, and the driver thereof.'

Under Eliseus

Eliseus divides the Jordan

2. Kings 2, 14

And he struck the waters with the mantle of Elias, that had fallen from him, and they were not divided. And he said: 'Where is now the God of Elias?'

And he struck the waters, and they were divided, hither and thither, and Eliseus passed over.

Eliseus heals the bitter Water

2. Kings 2, 19 - 22

And the men of the city said to Eliseus: 'Behold the situation of this city is very good, as thou, my lord, seest: but the waters are very bad, and the ground barren.'

And he said: 'Bring me a new vessel, and put salt into it.'

And when they had brought it, he went out to the spring of the waters, and cast the salt into it, and said: 'Thus saith the Lord: I have healed these waters, and there shall be no more in them death or barrenness.'

And the waters were healed unto this day, according to the word of Eliseus, which he spoke.

Two mocking Boys ripped apart by two Bears

2. Kings 2, 23 - 24

And he went up from thence to Bethel: and as he was going up by the way, little boys came out of the city and mocked him, saying: 'Go up, thou bald head; go up, thou bald head.'

And looking back, he saw them, and cursed them in the name of the Lord: and there came forth two bears out of the forest, and tore of them two and forty boys.

The Country was filled with Water without Rain

2. Kings 3, 15 - 20

But now bring me hither a minstrel. And when the minstrel played, the hand of the Lord came upon him, and he said:

'Thus saith the Lord: Make the channel of this torrent full of ditches. For thus saith the Lord: You shall not see wind, nor rain: and yet this channel shall be filled with waters, and you shall drink, you and your families, and your beasts. And this is a small thing in the sight of the Lord: moreover he will deliver also Moab into your hands.

And you shall destroy every fenced city, and every choice city, and shall cut down every fruitful tree, and shall stop up all the springs of waters, and every goodly field you shall cover with stones.'

And it came to pass in the morning, when the sacrifices used to be offered, that behold, water came by the way of Edom, and the country was filled with water.

Oil of the Window increased

2. Kings 4, 1 - 7

Now a certain woman of the wives of the prophets cried to Eliseus, saying: 'Thy servant my husband is dead, and thou knowest that thy servant was one that feared God, and behold the creditor is come to take away my two sons to serve him.'

And Eliseus said to her: 'What wilt thou have me to do for thee? Tell me, what hast thou in thy house?'

And she answered: 'I thy handmaid have nothing in my house but a little oil, to anoint me.'

And he said to her: 'Go, borrow of all thy neighbours empty vessels not a few. And go in, and shut thy door, when thou art within, and thy sons: and pour out thereof into all those vessels: and when they are full take them away.'

So the woman went, and shut the door upon her, and upon her sons: they brought her the vessels, and she poured in. And when the vessels were full, she said to her son: 'Bring me yet a vessel.'

And he answered: 'I have no more.'

And the oil stood.

And she came, and told the man of God. And he said: 'Go, sell the oil, and pay thy creditor: and thou and thy sons live of the rest.'

Son of the Widow of Sunem awoke from the Dead

2. Kings 4, 32 - 37

Eliseus therefore went into the house, and behold the child lay dead on his bed. And going in he shut the door upon him, and upon the child, and prayed to the Lord. And he went up, and lay upon the child: and he put his mouth upon his mouth, and his eyes upon his eyes, and his hands upon his hands: and he bowed himself upon him, and the child's flesh grew warm.

Then he returned and walked in the house, once to and from: and he went up, and lay upon him: and the child gaped seven times, and opened his eyes.

And he called Giezi, and said to him: 'Call this Sunamitess.'

And she being called, went in to him: and he said: 'Take up thy son.'

She came and fell at his feet, and worshipped upon the ground: and took up her son, and went out.

A deadly Meal becomes edible

2. Kings 4, 38 - 41

And Eliseus returned to Galgal, and there was a famine in the land, and the sons of the prophets dwelt before him. And he said to one of his servants: 'Set on the great pot, and boil pottage for the sons of the prophets.'

And one went out into the field to gather wild herbs: and he found something like a wild vine, and gathered of it wild gourds of the field, and filled his mantle, and coming back he shred them into the pot of pottage, for he knew not what it was.

And they poured it out for their companions to eat: and when they had tasted of the pottage, they cried out, saying: 'Death is in the pot, O man of God.' And they could not eat thereof.

But he said: 'Bring some meal.'

And when they had brought it, he cast it into the pot, and said: Pour out for the people, that they may eat.

And there was now no bitterness in the pot.

Hundret Man ate from twenty Leaves of Barley

2. Kings 4, 42 - 44

And a certain man came from Baalsalisa bringing to the man of God bread of the firstfruits, twenty leaves of barley, and new corn in his scrip. And he said: 'Give to the people, that they may eat.'

And his servant answered him: 'How much is this, that I should set it before a hundred men?'

He said again: 'Give to the people, that they may eat: for thus saith the Lord: They shall eat, and there shall be left.'

So he set it before them: and they ate, and there was left according to the word of the Lord.

Naaman was made clean

2. Kings 5, 10 - 14

And Eliseus sent a messenger to him, saying: 'Go, and wash seven times in the Jordan, and thy flesh shall recover health, and thee shalt be clean.'

Naaman was angry and went away, saying: 'I thought he would hare come out to me, and standing would hare invoked the name of the Lord his God, and touched with his hand the place of the leprosy, and healed me. Are not the Abana, and the Pharphar, rivers of Damascus, better than all the waters of Israel, that I may wash in them, and be made clean?'

So as he turned, and was going away with indignation,

His servants came to him, and said to him: 'Father, if the prophet had bid thee do some great thing, surely thou shouldst have done it: how much rather what he now hath said to thee: Wash, and thou shalt he clean?'

Then he went down, and washed in the Jordan seven times: according to the word of the man of God, and his flesh was restored, like the flesh of a little child, and he was made clean.

Giezi becomes a Leper

2. Kings 5, 26 - 27

But he said: 'Was not my heart present, when the man turned back from his chariot to meet thee? So now thou hast received money, and received garments, to buy oliveyards, and vineyards, and sheep, and oxen, and menservants, and maidservants.'

But the leprosy of Naaman shall also stick to thee, and to thy seed for ever.

And he went out from him a leper as white as snow.

Iron swims

2. Kings 6, 6

And the man of God said: 'Where did it fall?' and he shewed him the place.

Then he cut off a piece of wood, and cast it in thither: and the iron swam.

The Army of the Syrians becomes blind and sees again

2. Kings 6, 18 - 20

And the enemies came down to him, but Eliseus prayed to the Lord, saying: 'Strike, I beseech thee, this people with blindness.'

And the Lord struck them with blindness, according to the word of Eliseus.

And Eliseus said to them: 'This is not the way, neither is this the city: follow me, and I will shew you the man whom you seek.'

So he led them into Samaria. And when they were come into Samaria, Eliseus said: 'Lord, open the eyes of these men, that they may see.'

And the Lord opened their eyes, and they saw themselves to be in the midst of Samaria.

The LORD defeats the Besiegers of Samaria

2. Kings 7

And Eliseus said: 'Hear ye the word of the Lord: Thus saith the Lord: To morrow about this time a bushel of fine hour shall be sold for a stater, and two bushels of barley for a stater, in the gate of Samaria.'

Then one of the lords, upon whose hand the king leaned, answering the man of God, said: 'If the Lord should make flood-gates in heaven, can that possibly be which thou sayest?'

And he said: 'Thou shalt see it with thy eyes, but shalt not eat thereof.'

Now there were four lepers, at the entering in of the gate: and they said one to another: 'What mean we to stay here till we die? If we will enter into the city, we shall die with the famine: and if we will remain here, we must also die: come, therefore, and let us run over to the camp of the Syrians. If they spare us, we shall live: but if they kill us, we shall but die.'

So they arose in the evening, to go to the Syrian camp, And when they were come to the first part of the camp of the Syrians, they found no man there. For the Lord had made them hear, in the camp of Syria, the noise of chariots, and of horses, and of a very great army, and they said one to another: 'Behold the king of Israel hath hired against us the kings of the Hethites, and of the Egyptians, and they are come upon us.'

Wherefore they arose, and fled away in the dark, and left their tents, and their horses and asses in the camp, and fled, desiring to save their lives.

So when these lepers were come to the beginning of the camp, they went into one tent, and ate and drank: and they took from thence silver, and gold, and raiment, and went, and hid it: and they came again, and went into another tent, and carried from thence in like manner, and hid it.

Then they said one to another: 'We do not well: for this is a day of good tidings. If we hold our peace, and do not tell it till the morning, we shall be charged with a crime: come, let us go and tell it in the king's court.'

So they came to the gate of the city, and told them, saying: 'We went to the camp of the Syrians, and we found no man there, but horses, and asses tied, and the tents standing.'

Then the guards of the gate went, and told it within the king's palace.

And he arose in the night and said to his servants: 'I tell you what the Syrians have done to us: They know that we suffer great famine, and therefore they are gone out of the camp, and lie hid in the fields, saying: - When they come out of the city we shall take them alive, and then we may get into the city.-'

And one of his servants answered: 'Let us take the five horses that are remaining in the city (because there are no more in the whole multitude of Israel, for the rest are consumed,) and let us send and see.'

They brought therefore two horses, and the king sent into the camp of the Syrians, saying: 'Go, and see.'

And they went after them as far as the Jordan: and behold all the way was full of garments, and vessels, which the Syrians had cast away in their fright, and the messengers returned and told the king.

And the people going out pillaged the camp of the Syrians: and a bushel of fine flour was sold for a stater, and two bushels of barley for a stater, according to the word of the Lord.

And the king appointed that lord on whose hand he leaned, to stand at the gate: and the people trod upon him in the entrance of the gate; and he died, as the man of God had said, when the king came down to him.

And it came to pass according to the word of the man of God, which he spoke to the king, when he said: 'Two bushels of barley shall be for a stater, and a bushel of fine flour for a stater, at this very time to morrow in the gate of Samaria.'

When that lord answered the man of God, and said: 'Although the Lord should make floodgates in heaven, could this come to pass which thou sayest?'

And he said to him: 'Thou shalt see with thy eyes, and shalt not eat thereof.'

And so it fell out to him as it was foretold, and the people trod upon him in the gate, and he died.

The Bones of Eliseus bring a Man back to Life

2. Kings 13, 20 - 21

And Eliseus died, and they buried him.

And the rovers from Moab came into the land the same year. And some that were burying a man, saw the rovers, and cast the body into the sepulchre of Eliseus. And when it had touched the bones of Eliseus, the man came to life, and stood upon his feet.

During the Time of the Babylonian Exile

*Three Friends are saved
from the fiery Oven*

Daniel 3, 19 - 27

Then was Nebuchadnezzar full of fury, and the form of his visage was changed against Shadrach, Meshach, and Abed-nego.

He spoke, and commanded that they should heat the furnace seven times more than it was wont to be heated. And he commanded the most mighty men that were in his army to bind Shadrach, Meshach, and Abed-nego, and cast them into the burning fiery furnace.

Then these men were bound in their hosen, their tunics, and their cloaks, and their garments, and were cast into the midst of the burning fiery furnace. Forasmuch as the king's commandment was rigorous, and the furnace exceeding hot, the flame of the fire slew those men that had taken up Shadrach, Meshach, and Abed-nego. And these three men, Shadrach, Meshach, and Abed-nego, fell down bound into the midst of the burning fiery furnace.

Then Nebuchadnezzar the king was astonied, and rose up in haste; he spoke and said unto his counsellors, 'Did not we cast three men bound into the midst of the fire?'

They answered and said to the king, 'True, O king.'

He answered and said, 'Lo, I see four men loose, walking in the midst of the fire, and they have no hurt; and the appearance of the fourth is like a son of God.'

Then Nebuchadnezzar came near to the opening of the burning fiery furnace; he spoke and said, 'Shadrach, Meshach, and Abed-nego, ye servants of the Most High God, come forth, and come [hither].'

Then Shadrach, Meshach, and Abed-nego came forth from the midst of the fire.

And the satraps, the prefects, and the governors, and the king's counsellors, being gathered together, saw these men, upon whose bodies the fire had had no power, nor was the hair of their head singed, neither were their hosen changed, nor had the smell of fire passed on them.

(from the Darby Translation. Please compare this Chapter to the Douay-Reims 1899 Translation)

Daniel was protected from the Lions

Daniel 6, 16 - 25

Then the king commanded, and they brought Daniel, and cast him into the den of the lions. And the king said to Daniel: 'Thy God, whom thou always servest, he will deliver thee.'

And a stone was brought, and laid upon the mouth of the den: which the king sealed with his own ring, and with the ring of his nobles, that nothing should be done against Daniel. And the king went away to his house and laid himself down without taking supper, and meat was not set before him, and even sleep departed from him.

Then the king rising very early in the morning, went in haste to the lions' den: And coming near to the den, cried with a lamentable voice to Daniel, and said to him: 'Daniel, servant of the living God, hath thy God, whom thou servest always, been able, thinkest thou, to deliver thee from the lions?'

And Daniel answering the king, said: 'O king, live for ever: My God hath sent his angel, and hath shut up the mouths of the lions, and they have not hurt me: forasmuch as before him justice hath been found in me: yea and before thee, O king, I have done no offence.'

Then was the king exceeding glad for him, and he commanded that Daniel should be taken out of the den: and Daniel was taken out of the den, and no hurt was found in him, because he believed in his God.

And by the king's commandment, those men were brought that had accused Daniel: and they were cast into the lions' den, they and their children, and their wives: and they did not reach the bottom of the den, before the lions caught them, and broke all their bones in pieces.

Then king Darius wrote to all people, tribes, and languages, dwelling in the whole earth: PEACE be multiplied unto you.

From the New Testament

A Stater in the Mouth of a Fish

Matthew 17, 23 - 26

And when they were come to Capharnaum, they that received the didrachmas, came to Peter and said to him: 'Doth not your master pay the didrachmas?'

He said: 'Yes.'

And when he was come into the house, Jesus prevented him, saying: 'What is thy opinion, Simon? The kings of the earth, of whom do they receive tribute or custom? of their own children, or of strangers?'

And he said: 'Of strangers.'

Jesus said to him: 'Then the children are free.

But that we may not scandalize them, go to the sea, and cast in a hook: and that fish which shall first come up, take: and when thou hast opened its mouth, thou shalt find a stater: take that, and give it to them for me and thee.'

The great Fishing

Luke 5, 1 - 11

And it came to pass, that when the multitudes pressed upon him to hear the word of God, he stood by the lake of Genesareth, And saw two ships standing by the lake: but the fishermen were gone out of them, and were washing their nets.

And going into one of the ships that was Simon's, he desired him to draw back a little from the land. And sitting he taught the multitudes out of the ship.

Now when he had ceased to speak, he said to Simon: 'Launch out into the deep, and let down your nets for a draught.'

And Simon answering said to him: 'Master, we have labored all the night, and have taken nothing: but at thy word I will let down the net.'

And when they had done this, they enclosed a very great multitude of fishes, and their net broke.

And they beckoned to their partners that were in the other ship, that they should come and help them.

And they came, and filled both the ships, so that they were almost sinking. Which when Simon Peter saw, he fell down at Jesus' knees, saying: 'Depart from me, for I am a sinful man, O Lord.'

For he was wholly astonished, and all that were with him, at the draught of the fishes which they had taken. And so were also James and John the sons of Zebedee, who were Simon's partners. And Jesus saith to Simon: 'Fear not: from henceforth thou shalt catch men.'

And having brought their ships to land, leaving all things, they followed him.

Jesus heals the Ear of Malchus

Luke 22, 49 - 51

And they that were about him, seeing what would follow, said to him: 'Lord, shall we strike with the sword?'

And one of them struck the servant of the high priest, and cut off his right ear. But Jesus answering, said: 'Suffer ye thus far.'

And when he had touched his ear, he healed him. (1)

The Transformation from Water into Wine

John 2, 1 - 11

And the third day, there was a marriage in Cana of Galilee: and the mother of Jesus was there. And Jesus also was invited, and his disciples, to the marriage. And the wine failing, the mother of Jesus saith to him: 'They have no wine.'

And Jesus saith to her: 'Woman, what is that to me and to thee? my hour is not yet come.'

His mother saith to the waiters: 'Whatsoever he shall say to you, do ye.'

Now there were set there six waterpots of stone, according to the manner of the purifying of the Jews, containing two or three measures apiece. Jesus saith to them: 'Fill the waterpots with water.'

And they filled them up to the brim.

And Jesus saith to them: 'Draw out now, and carry to the chief steward of the feast.'

And they carried it.

And when the chief steward had tasted the water made wine, and knew not whence it was, but the waiters knew who had drawn the water; the chief steward calleth the bridegroom, And saith to him: 'Every man at first setteth forth good wine, and when men have well drunk, then that which is worse. But thou hast kept the good wine until now.'

This beginning of miracles did Jesus in Cana of Galilee; and manifested his glory, and his disciples believed in him.

Catching a Multitude of Fishes

John 21, 1 - 14

After this, Jesus shewed himself again to the disciples at the sea of Tiberias. And he shewed himself after this manner. There were together Simon Peter, and Thomas, who is called Didymus, and Nathanael, who was of Cana of Galilee, and the sons of Zebedee, and two others of his disciples. Simon Peter saith to them: 'I go a fishing.'

They say to him: 'We also come with thee.'

And they went forth, and entered into the ship: and that night they caught nothing. But when the morning was come, Jesus stood on the shore: yet the disciples knew not that it was Jesus.

Jesus therefore said to them: 'Children, have you any meat?'

They answered him: 'No.'

He saith to them: 'Cast the net on the right side of the ship, and you shall find.'

They cast therefore; and now they were not able to draw it, for the multitude of fishes. That disciple therefore whom Jesus loved, said to Peter: 'It is the Lord.'

Simon Peter, when he heard that it was the Lord, girt his coat about him, (for he was naked,) and cast himself into the sea. But the other disciples came in the ship, (for they were not far from the land, but as it were two hundred cubits,) dragging the net with fishes.

As soon then as they came to land, they saw hot coals lying, and a fish laid thereon, and bread. Jesus saith to them: 'Bring hither of the fishes which you have now caught.'

Simon Peter went up, and drew the net to land, full of great fishes, one hundred and fifty-three. And although there were so many, the net was not broken. Jesus saith to them: 'Come, and dine.'

And none of them who were at meat, durst ask him: 'Who art thou?' knowing that it was the Lord.

And Jesus cometh and taketh bread, and giveth them, and fish in like manner.

This is now the third time that Jesus was manifested to his disciples, after he was risen from the dead.

The Feeding of 4000

Matthew 15, 32 - 38

And Jesus called together his disciples, and said: 'I have compassion on the multitudes, because they continue with me now three days, and have not what to eat, and I will not send them away fasting, lest they faint in the way.'

And the disciples say unto him: 'Whence then should we have so many loaves in the desert, as to fill so great a multitude?'

And Jesus said to them: 'How many loaves have you?'

But they said: 'Seven, and a few little fishes.'

And he commanded the multitude to sit down upon the ground. And taking the seven loaves and the fishes, and giving thanks, he brake, and gave to his disciples, and the disciples to the people.

And they did all eat, and had their fill. And they took up seven baskets full, of what remained of the fragments. And they that did eat, were four thousand men, beside children and women.

Mark 8, 1 - 9

In those days again, when there was a great multitude, and had nothing to eat; calling his disciples together, he saith to them: 'I have compassion on the multitude, for behold they have now been with me three days, and have nothing to eat. And if I shall send them away fasting to their home, they will faint in the way; for some of them came from afar off.'

And his disciples answered him: 'From whence can any one fill them here with bread in the wilderness?'

And he asked them: 'How many loaves have ye?'

Who said: 'Seven.'

And taking the seven loaves, giving thanks, he broke, and gave to his disciples for to set before them; and they set them before the people.

And they had a few little fishes; and he blessed them, and commanded them to be set before them. And they did eat and were filled; and they took up that which was left of the fragments, seven baskets.

And they that had eaten were about four thousand; and he sent them away.

A Fig Tree withered

Matthew 21, 18 - 22

And in the morning, returning into the city, he was hungry. And seeing a certain fig tree by the way side, he came to it, and found nothing on it but leaves only, and he saith to it: 'May no fruit grow on thee henceforward for ever.'

And immediately the fig tree withered away.

And the disciples seeing it wondered, saying: 'How is it presently withered away?'

And Jesus answering, said to them: 'Amen, I say to you, if you shall have faith, and stagger not, not only this of the fig tree shall you do, but also if you shall say to this mountain, Take up and cast thyself into the sea, it shall be done.

And in all things whatsoever you shall ask in prayer, believing, you shall receive.'

Mark 11, 12 - 24

And the next day when they came out from Bethania, he was hungry. And when he had seen afar off a fig tree having leaves, he came if perhaps he might find any thing on it. And when he was come to it, he found nothing but leaves. For it was not the time for figs. And answering he said to it: 'May no man hereafter eat fruit of thee any more for ever.'

And his disciples heard it.

And they came to Jerusalem. And when he was entered into the temple, he began to cast out them that sold and bought in the temple, and overthrew the tables of the money-changers, and the chairs of them that sold doves. And he suffered not that any man should carry a vessel through the temple;

And he taught, saying to them: 'Is it not written, My house shall be called the house of prayer to all nations? But you have made it a den of thieves.'

Which when the chief priests and the scribes had heard, they sought how they might destroy him. For they feared him, because the whole multitude was in admiration at his doctrine.

And when evening was come, he went forth out of the city. And when they passed by in the morning they saw the fig tree dried up from the roots. And Peter remembering, said to him: 'Rabbi, behold the fig tree, which thou didst curse, is withered away.'

And Jesus answering, saith to them: 'Have the faith of God. Amen I say to you, that whosoever shall say to this mountain, Be thou removed and be cast into the sea, and shall not stagger in his heart, but believe, that whatsoever he saith shall be done; it shall be done unto him.

Therefore I say unto you, all things, whatsoever you ask when ye pray, believe that you shall receive; and they shall come unto you.'

A Storm was calmed

Matthew 8, 23 - 27

And when he entered into the boat, his disciples followed him: And behold a great tempest arose in the sea, so that the boat was covered with waves, but he was asleep. And they came to him, and awaked him, saying: 'Lord, save us, we perish.'

And Jesus saith to them: 'Why are you fearful, O ye of little faith?'

Then rising up he commanded the winds, and the sea, and there came a great calm.

But the men wondered, saying: 'What manner of man is this, for the winds and the sea obey him?'

Mark 4, 36 - 41

And he saith to them that day, when evening was come: Let us pass over to the other side. And sending away the multitude, they take him even as he was in the ship: and there were other ships with him.

And there arose a great storm of wind, and the waves beat into the ship, so that the ship was filled. And he was in the hinder part of the ship, sleeping upon a pillow; and they awake him, and say to him: 'Master, doth it not concern thee that we perish?'

And rising up, he rebuked the wind, and said to the sea: 'Peace, be still.'

And the wind ceased: and there was made a great calm. And he said to them: 'Why are you fearful? have you not faith yet?'

And they feared exceedingly: and they said one to another: 'Who is this (thinkest thou) that both wind and sea obey him?'

Luke 8, 22 - 25

And it came to pass on a certain day that he went into a little ship with his disciples, and he said to them: Let us go over to the other side of the lake. And they launched forth.

And when they were sailing, he slept; and there came down a storm of wind upon the lake, and they were filled, and were in danger. And they came and awaked him, saying: 'Master, we perish.'

But he arising, rebuked the wind and the rage of the water; and it ceased, and there was a calm. And he said to them: 'Where is your faith?'

Who being afraid, wondered, saying one to another: 'Who is this, (think you), that he commandeth both the winds and the sea, and they obey him?'

Waking on the Water

Matthew 14, 22 - 33

And forthwith Jesus obliged his disciples to go up into the boat, and to go before him over the water, till he dismissed the people. And having dismissed the multitude, he went into a mountain alone to pray. And when it was evening, he was there alone.

But the boat in the midst of the sea was tossed with the waves: for the wind was contrary. And in the fourth watch of the night, he came to them walking upon the sea. And they seeing him walk upon the sea, were troubled, saying: 'It is an apparition.'

And they cried out for fear.

And immediately Jesus spoke to them, saying: 'Be of good heart: it is I, fear ye not.'

And Peter making answer, said: 'Lord, if it be thou, bid me come to thee upon the waters.'

And he said: 'Come.'

And Peter going down out of the boat, walked upon the water to come to Jesus.

But seeing the wind strong, he was afraid: and when he began to sink, he cried out, saying: 'Lord, save me.'

And immediately Jesus stretching forth his hand took hold of him, and said to him: 'O thou of little faith, why didst thou doubt?'

And when they were come up into the boat, the wind ceased.

And they that were in the boat came and adored him, saying: 'Indeed thou art the Son of God.'

Mark 6, 47 - 52

And when it was late, the ship was in the midst of the sea, and himself alone on the land. And seeing them labouring in rowing, (for the wind was against them,) and about the fourth watch of the night, he cometh to them walking upon the sea, and he would have passed by them.

But they seeing him walking upon the sea, thought it was an apparition, and they cried out. For they all saw him, and were troubled.

And immediately he spoke with them, and said to them: 'Have a good heart, it is I, fear ye not.'

And he went up to them into the ship, and the wind ceased: and they were far more astonished within themselves:

For they understood not concerning the loaves; for their heart was blinded.

John 6, 16 - 21

And when evening was come, his disciples went down to the sea. And when they had gone up into a ship, they went over the sea to Capharnaum; and it was now dark, and Jesus was not come unto them. And the sea arose, by reason of a great wind that blew.

When they had rowed therefore about five and twenty or thirty furlongs, they see Jesus walking upon the sea, and drawing nigh to the ship, and they were afraid.

But he saith to them: 'It is I; be not afraid.'

They were willing therefore to take him into the ship; and presently the ship was at the land to which they were going.

5000 were fed

Matthew 14, 15 - 21

And when it was evening, his disciples came to him, saying: 'This is a desert place, and the hour is now past: send away the multitudes, that going into the towns, they may buy themselves victuals.'

But Jesus said to them, 'They have no need to go: give you them to eat.'

They answered him: 'We have not here, but five loaves, and two fishes.'

He said to them: 'Bring them hither to me.'

And when he had commanded the multitudes to sit down upon the grass, he took the five loaves and the two fishes, and looking up to heaven, he blessed, and brake, and gave the loaves to his disciples, and the disciples to the multitudes.

And they did all eat, and were filled.

And they took up what remained, twelve full baskets of fragments. And the number of them that did eat, was five thousand men, besides women and children.

Mark 6, 35 - 44

And when the day was now far spent, his disciples came to him, saying: 'This is a desert place, and the hour is now past: Send them away, that going into the next villages and towns, they may buy themselves meat to eat.'

And he answering said to them: 'Give you them to eat.'

And they said to him: 'Let us go and buy bread for two hundred pence, and we will give them to eat.'

And he saith to them: 'How many loaves have you? go and see. And when they knew, they say: 'Five, and two fishes.'

And he commanded them that they should make them all sit down by companies upon the green grass. And they sat down in ranks, by hundreds and by fifties. And when he had taken the five loaves, and the two fishes: looking up to heaven, he blessed, and broke the loaves, and gave to his disciples to set before them: and the two fishes he divided among them all.

And they all did eat, and had their fill. And they took up the leavings, twelve full baskets of fragments, and of the fishes.

And they that did eat, were five thousand men.

Luke 9, 12 - 17

Now the day began to decline. And the twelve came and said to him: 'Send away the multitude, that going into the towns and villages round about, they may lodge and get victuals; for we are here in a desert place.'

But he said to them: 'Give you them to eat.'

And they said: 'We have no more than five loaves and two fishes; unless perhaps we should go and buy food for all this multitude.'

Now there were about five thousand men. And he said to his disciples: 'Make them sit down by fifties in a company.'

And they did so; and made them all sit down.

And taking the five loaves and the two fishes, he looked up to heaven, and blessed them; and he broke, and distributed to his disciples, to set before the multitude.

And they did all eat, and were filled.

And there were taken up of fragments that remained to them, twelve baskets.

John 6, 5 - 14

When Jesus therefore had lifted up his eyes, and seen that a very great multitude cometh to him, he said to Philip: 'Whence shall we buy bread, that these may eat?'

And this he said to try him; for he himself knew what he would do.

Philip answered him: 'Two hundred pennyworth of bread is not sufficient for them, that every one may take a little.'

One of his disciples, Andrew, the brother of Simon Peter, saith to him: 'There is a boy here that hath five barley loaves, and two fishes; but what are these among so many?'

Then Jesus said: 'Make the men sit down.'

Now there was much grass in the place. The men therefore sat down, in number about five thousand. And Jesus took the loaves: and when he had given thanks, he distributed to them that were set down. In like manner also of the fishes, as much as they would.

And when they were filled, he said to his disciples: 'Gather up the fragments that remain, lest they be lost.'

They gathered up therefore, and filled twelve baskets with the fragments of the five barley loaves, which remained over and above to them that had eaten.

Now those men, when they had seen what a miracle Jesus had done, said: 'This is of a truth the prophet, that is to come into the world.'

Register

(1) also see the Book:

> *The Healing Miracles of Jesus*
> *Healing Miracles of the Apostles*
> and a Message to the Believers.

Further Information in the Appendix.

Thanks and Inspiration

To this wonderful Project I was inspired by

The International School of Ministries

on which I just stared my Studies when the Idea to this Book came to me. The Lectures of the first Semester already touched me so deeply and found such Resonance inside of me, that I could finish this work very quickly - which basically contains the Lectures of the second Course of the first Semester.

The International School of Ministries teaches in many different Languages and builds on inspiring Teachers and Preachers from all Continents. This School offers to every Seeker not just a Guideline, but a deep Understanding of what the real Believe in our Lord Jesus Christ really contains, what it includes and to what it enables.

May God strengthen many more People in their Believe through the International School of Ministries and let them find Jesus in their Hearts.

ISOM Bible School

www.isom.org

About the Author

www.antonia-katharina.de

www.bolonka-zucht.de

www.light-in-time.com

Youtube Kanal:
Antonia Katharina
aus dem Alten Jagdhaus

More Books of Antonia Katharina Tessnow

The Books of the Bible as separate, single Books in big Writing

Why the books of the Bible as separate singles? The reason is as simple as practical: Most of the time, the Bible in its entirety has a very small writing and is, therefore, hard to read. Even if the publication itself is as big as possible and the writing still hardly decent, it is practically impossible to carry around all day, ever since it is so heavy.

But the books of the Bible, published as single books, allows the writing to be nice and big and therefore easy to read. Instead of carrying a heavy, big book around, you can choose one book of your liking, light enough to put in every pocket and easy to read. This way you can read the Bible wherever you like. In other words: The translators made the Bible available, this version makes it possible to easily read it.

Additionally, the single and easy-to-read versions of the single, biblical books can serve as an entry into the most important book of all times. Also the different books can be given away as a present to friends, family and loved ones. The easy-to-read version of the Bible is not only perfect for all those, whose hearts the message of salvation already reached, but also for all those who did not yet dare to approach the Bible and possibly felt overwhelmed by the volume and length of it.

The message of the Holy Scriptures can be of great help and support, give confidence, bring hope, comfort you, show sympathy and give consolation, especially during times, when we need hope and consolation so very much.

Whoever is seeking for the way home should know, that it is always open and there for us. This way is shown and can be found through the Bible. By making the decision to open up for the message of the Holy Scriptures, many people, throughout centuries, have found salvation, safety, hope and peace. And that is true up to this day.

Writing, Format, Layout:
Antonia Katharina Tessnow

www.antonia-katharina.de

This Project is available
in German and English

The Healing Miracles of Jesus
Healing Miracles of the Apostles
and a Message to all Believers

Now there are diversities of gifts, but the same Spirit. And there are differences of administrations, but the same Lord. And there are diversities of operations, but it is the same God which worketh all in all.

But the manifestation of the Spirit is given to every man to profit withal. For to one is given by the Spirit the word of wisdom; to another the word of knowledge by the same Spirit; To another faith by the same Spirit; to another the gifts of healing by the same Spirit;

To another the working of miracles; to another prophecy; to another discerning of spirits; to another divers kinds of tongues; to another the interpretation of tongues:

But all these worketh that one and the selfsame Spirit, dividing to every man severally as he will.

1. Corinthians 12, 4 - 11

As each has received a gift, employ it in serving one another, as good managers of the grace of God in its various forms.

1. Peter 4, 10

Could Jesus really heal? What is his Message to us? To what are we - through our Confession to him and our Discipleship - commissioned? This Book is a Composition of a Variety of Bible-Verses which give Answers to all such Questions.

Jesus' Love for Animals

Christian Inspirations from the Gospel of the Holy Twelve

Jesus Christ did not only teach us love for our humanly brothers and sisters, but also for our loyal, loving and tenderhearted companions, the animals.

The excerpts from the Gospel of the Holy Twelve, also known as the

Gospel of the Nazarenes

allow deep insights into the commands of our Savior, that is to confront our brothers and sisters, the animals, with love and treat them with full compassion. To everyone, who hopes to find orientation and to step safely through life: it is absolutely worth to align your being based on the teachings and commands of Jesus Christ, for he is and has always been the way.

Furthermore, a short attachment gives some understanding about the philosophy of other religions and writers, who also clearly confess their love of animals.

Holy Night
Silent Night

1943. It is Christmas. All around the world, children write diaries to somehow cope with the unbelievable experiences they are send through during wartimes and turmoil. The slightly older sister of Antonia Katharina's mother is 9 years old when she describes the events of one single night through her childish eyes. A destiny that leaves deep impressions on ones soul and won't leave anyone untouched.

A wonderful reminder of the peaceful times we are allowed to live in today.

Antonia Katharina Tessnow is the daughter of a former East Prussian Family who came to Germany after World War I. Her grandparents settled in Berlin but had to flee the city together with their children after their apartment building was bombed and completely destroyed during the last year of World War II. They returned many years later to Berlin, but even though Antonia Katharina was born there, she never felt at home in this city. Today she lives in the countryside of Mecklenburg-Vorpommern.

Madras
Magic of the Palm Leafs

This Book is available in English and German

The Palm Leaf Library - Thousands of years old and an unsolved secret until today. The mystery of this place is the key subject of 'Madras'. The true story evolves around one of the greatest secrets of mankind.

I have been there. I left my small hometown near Berlin and discovered a legend which says, that every life story is written on a palm leaf; every life story? No, but the live story of all those people, who will undergo the long travel to one of the libraries and search for it. That is what I have done.

And this is, what I have found.

People who have read this book:

'A fascinating book. Whoever wants to find the answer to the question: How many lives do we have? will find it here.'

Günther Prinz, Managing Director and Chief Editor of 'Bild', Germany.

'So there is my entire life written on a Palm Leaf in Madras! This book completely changed my understanding of time and space.'

Fritz Bloomberg, Ex-Vicepresident Burda Press, New York

'Mind blowing! The ideal book for everybody who wants to learn about the unbelievable truth behind our existence.'

Gregor Tessnow, Germany

Author of the bestseller and the script of 'Knallhart'

Ebenfalls von der Autorin erhältlich:

Heilbehandlungen für Dich und Dein geliebtes Tier

*Erinnere Dich
an Deine verborgenen Fähigkeiten*

Bolonka Zwetna

*Von der Empfindsamkeit der Hundeseele
und der Liebe, die sie schenkt*

Kommunikation mit Tieren

ein Essay

Die Botschaft der Tiere

Der Weg zurück zu uns selbst

Ein Wegweiser durch unsere Zeit

Augen auf beim Welpenkauf

*Wissenswerte Tipps aus der Bolonka Zwetna
Hundezucht aus dem Alten Jagdhaus*

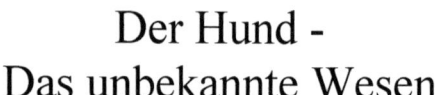

Der Hund -
Das unbekannte Wesen

Was Sie tun können,
damit Ihr Hunde Sie liebt

*Ein Leitfaden zur Eingewöhnung
des Hundes in ein neues Heim*

Celtic Spirit

*Eine Reise in die Tiefen
zeitloser keltischer Weisheit*

HAIR

Alles über alternative Haarpflege

Sternenstaub am Horizont

oder

Breakable - Zerbrechlich
der Fall

zwischen Selbstwert und Vernichtung

Breakable - Zerbrechlich

Der Skandalroman aus Mecklenburg

Nichts geschieht umsonst auf dieser Welt

der Fall
Breakable - Zerbrechlich
die Anhänge

Tattoo – Laser – Cover Up

Wenn der Traum zum Albtraum wird

Weiß Du, was Du mit Dir trägst?

*Eine Entscheidungshilfe
für Tattoo und Motiv*

Stille Nacht, Heilige Nacht

Erinnerungen an einen Heiligen Abend
in den letzten Tagen des zweiten Weltkriegs

eine Kurzgeschichte

Diese Geschichte
liegt in deutscher und Englischer Fassung vor.

Winston

Eine Pferdebuch-Trilogie für Jugendliche

*Der große Sammelband
mit allen 3 Bänden*

Ein Fohlen erblickt die Welt

Die große Show

Nichts ist unmöglich

Copyright of the Original by

Antonia Katharina Tessnow

ALL RIGHTS RESERVED. No part of this book may be reproduced in any form or by any electronic or mechanical means including information storage and retrieval systems without permission in writing from the publisher, except by reviewers who may quote brief passages in a review.